The
Oxford Book
Of English Verse
1250–1918